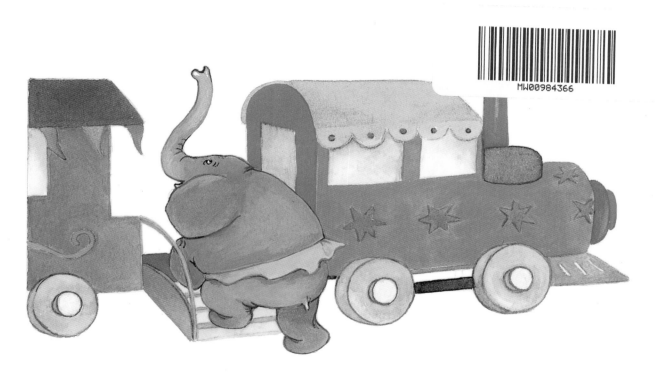

The elephant got on the train.

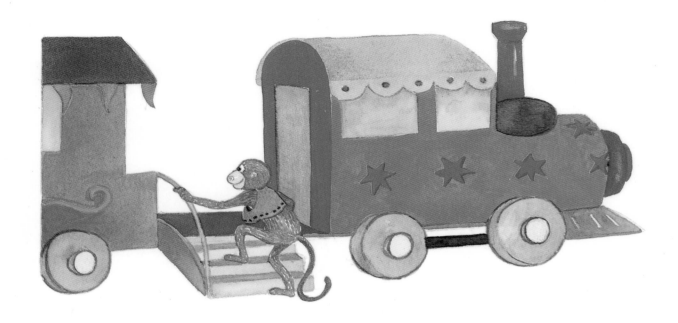

The monkey got on the train.

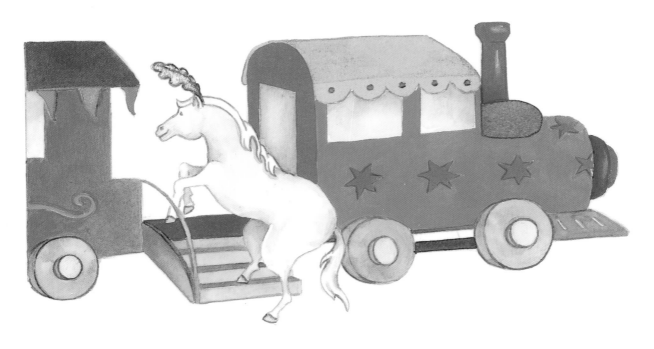

The horse got on the train.

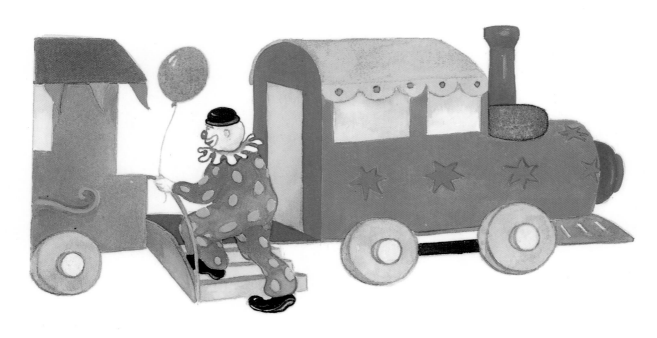

The clown got on the train.

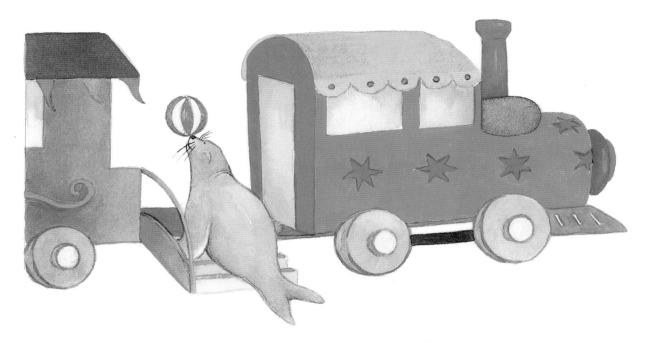

The seal got on the train.

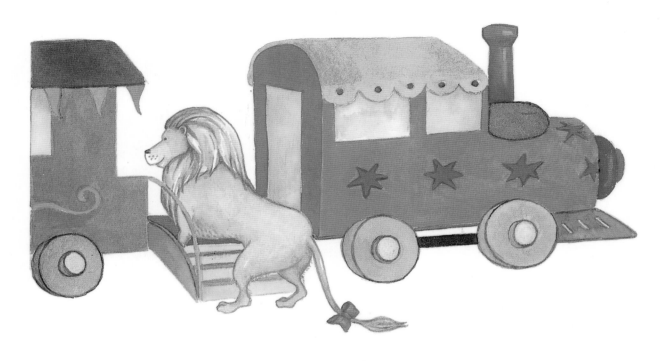

The lion got on the train.

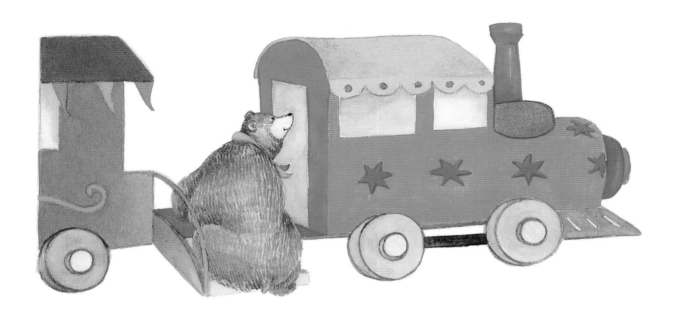

The bear got on the train.

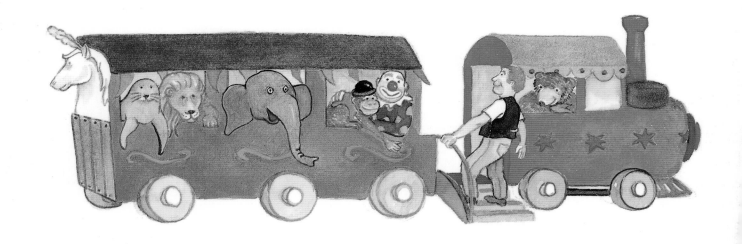

The man got on the train.